D0516110

Introducing Continents

South America

Anita Ganeri

Chicago, Illinois

© 2014 Heinemann Library
an imprint of Capstone Global Library, LLC
Chicago, Illinois

To contact Capstone Global Library please phone 800-747-4992, or visit our web site, www.capstonepub.com

Edited by Dan Nunn, Rebecca Rissman, Sian Smith, and Helen Cox Cannons
Designed by Philippa Jenkins
Original illustrations © Capstone Global Library Ltd 2014
Picture research by Liz Alexander and Tristan Leverett
Production by Vicki Fitzgerald
Originated by Capstone Global Library Ltd
Printed and bound in China by Leo Paper Products Ltd

17 16 15 14 13
10 9 8 7 6 5 4 3 2 1

Library of Congress Cataloging-in-Publication Data
Ganeri, Anita, 1961-
   Introducing South America / Anita Ganeri.
      pages cm. —(Introducing continents)
   Includes bibliographical references and index.
   ISBN 978-1-4329-8044-3 (hb)—ISBN 978-1-4329-8052-8 (pb) 1. South America—Juvenile literature. I. Title.

   F2208.5.G35 2013
   980—dc23   2012049500

54100465 4/14

Acknowledgments
The author and publisher are grateful to the following for permission to reproduce copyright material: Alamy p. 16 (© Les Gibbon); Corbis pp. 7 (© Johannes Mann), 18 (© Kit Houghton), 23 (© Peter M. Wilson); Getty Images pp. 14 (Paul Souders/The Image Bank), 22 (Alejandro Pagni/AFP); naturepl.com p. 17 (© Juan Manuel Borrero); Science Photo Library pp. 9 (Jacques Jangoux), 10 (Jacques Jangoux); Shutterstock pp. 6 (© Andrés Cuenca), 8 (© Natursports), 11 (© colacat), 12 (© XuRa), 13 (© Peter Zaharov), 15 (© Rechitan Sorin), 26 (© cifotart); SuperStock pp. 19 (Jan Sochor/age footstock), 20 (Prisma), 21 (Tips Images), 25 (imagebroker.net), 27 (Michael &Amp Jennifer Lewis/National Geographic).

Cover image of a shaded relief map of South America reproduced with permission of Shutterstock (© AridOcean); images of the Amazon River, Brazil and carnival parade at the Sambodrome, Rio de Janeiro, Brazil reproduced with permission of SuperStock (© Steve Vidler, © Yadid Levy/age fotostock).

Every effort has been made to contact copyright holders of any material reproduced in this book. Any omissions will be rectified in subsequent printings if notice is given to the publisher.

Disclaimer
All the Internet addresses (URLs) given in this book were valid at the time of going to press. However, due to the dynamic nature of the Internet, some addresses may have changed, or sites may have changed or ceased to exist since publication. While the author and publisher regret any inconvenience this may cause readers, no responsibility for any such changes can be accepted by either the author or the publisher.

Contents

Some words are shown in bold, **like this**. You can find out what they mean by looking in the glossary.

About South America

A **continent** is a huge area of land. There are seven continents on Earth. This book is about the continent of South America. South America is the fourth biggest continent.

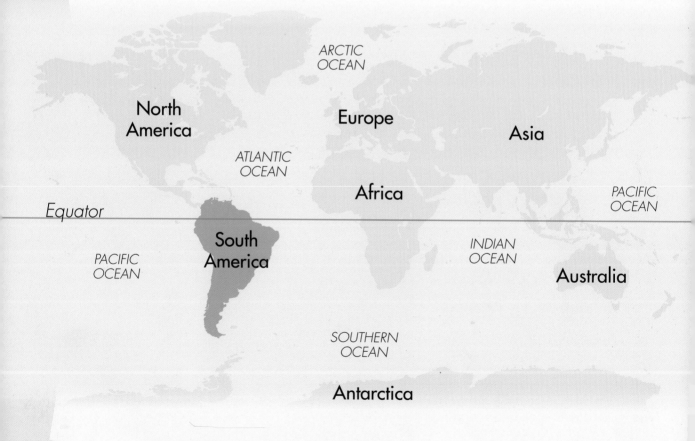

ARCTIC OCEAN

North America

Europe

Asia

ATLANTIC OCEAN

Africa

PACIFIC OCEAN

Equator

South America

INDIAN OCEAN

PACIFIC OCEAN

Australia

SOUTHERN OCEAN

Antarctica

South America is mostly surrounded by water. To the west is the Pacific Ocean. To the east is the Atlantic Ocean. A narrow strip of land links South America to the continent of North America.

South America Fact File	
Area	6,878,000 square miles (17,813,938 square kilometers)
Population	around 400 million
Number of countries	12
Highest mountain	Aconcagua at 22,831 feet (6,959 meters)
Longest river	Amazon at about 4,000 miles (6,437 kilometers)

Famous Places

There are many famous places in South America. Some are ancient. Machu Picchu is a ruined city high up in the Andes Mountains in Peru. It was built by the Inca people more than 500 years ago.

Tourists can visit the ruins of Machu Picchu high up in the mountains.

The statue's open arms are a sign of peace.

Some famous places are modern. A huge statue of Jesus Christ stands on top of a mountain near the city of Rio de Janeiro in Brazil. It is almost 130 feet (40 meters) tall and was built between 1922 and 1931.

Geography

South America has **grasslands**, rain forests, rivers, deserts, and mountains. The Andes is the world's longest **mountain range**. It runs for about 4,505 miles (7,250 kilometers) along the west coast of the **continent**.

Mount Cotopaxi in the Andes is an active volcano.

The Amazon rain forest is the biggest rain forest in the world.

Tropical rain forests cover about one-third of South America. The largest is the Amazon rain forest, which grows along the banks of the Amazon River in Brazil.

The mighty Amazon River is the longest river in South America. It is the second longest river on Earth. It begins in the Andes Mountains in Peru and flows across Peru and Brazil to the Atlantic Ocean.

The Amazon River flows into the sea off the coast of Brazil.

Angel Falls
Lake Guatavita
Amazon River
Sao Francisco River
Lake Titicaca
Lake Poopó
Uruguay River
Lake Chiquita
Lake Mirim
Negro River
Lake Buenos Aires

0   500 miles
0   800 km

Reeds make good materials for making boats on Lake Titicaca.

South America has many large lakes. Lake Titicaca is high up in the Andes Mountains. Tall **reeds** grow around the edges of the lake. Local people use the reeds to make huts and fishing boats.

Weather

South America has many different types of weather. It is hot and wet in the rain forests. The **grasslands** are hot and dry. It is even drier in the desert. Parts of the Atacama Desert in Chile have never had any rain.

The Atacama Desert is one of the driest places on Earth.

Ice and glaciers are found in the cold south of South America.

High up in the mountains, the weather gets very cold. It is also cold and windy at the southern tip of South America. In the winter, temperatures there can fall as low as -27 degrees Fahrenheit (-33 degrees Celsius).

Animals

An amazing number of animals live in South America. Andean **condors** soar above the mountains. Giant anteaters roam the **grasslands**. Huge tortoises live on the Galapagos Islands, off the west coast of Ecuador.

The Galapagos Islands are famous for their unusual wildlife.

Jaguars live in the Amazon rain forest. They are fierce hunters.

The Amazon rain forest is home to thousands of types of animals, such as jaguars, **capybaras**, and **anacondas**. There are also birds, lizards, monkeys, frogs, and insects. Many rain forest animals live in the treetops, where there is plenty of food to eat.

Plants

Many unusual plants grow in South America. The puya raimondii is a very rare plant that grows in the Andes Mountains. It only flowers once in its life, when it is between about 80 to 150 years old. Then the plant dies.

Puya raimondii flowers bloom on a giant stalk, which can be 33 feet (10 meters) tall.

roots

Orchid roots dangle down and collect water from the air.

Tall trees, such as brazil nut trees, grow in the rain forest. Beautiful orchids live high on the tree branches. Long vines twist around their trunks.

Natural Resources and Products

South America has many **natural resources**. In Argentina, the **grasslands** are used for farming. Farmers grow crops and keep cattle and sheep. These farms are some of the biggest in the world.

Huge herds of cattle graze on the grassland in Argentina.

This miner from Colombia is holding an emerald dug from the ground.

Many valuable products come from the rain forest, such as wood, brazil nuts, and palm oil. Oil comes from Venezuela. Copper and iron **ore** are **mined** in Chile. Colombia has coal mines and also produces precious emeralds.

People

About 380 million people live in South America. Some are **descended from** Europeans who settled in South America in the 1500s. Some are descended from people who lived in South America before the Europeans arrived.

Some people live in the rain forest, like this man from Venezuela.

This sign from Argentina is in Spanish.

Most people in South America speak Spanish. In Brazil, people speak Portuguese. Many ancient South American languages are also spoken. One of these is Quechua, which was the language of the Inca people.

Culture and Sports

Sports are very popular in South America, especially soccer. Brazil has won the soccer World Cup a record five times. Rio de Janeiro, in Brazil, is the home of the 2016 summer Olympic Games.

These soccer players are playing in the 2011 Copa America soccer tournament.

Carnival time in Rio is the highlight of the year!

Every year, in February or March, a world-famous carnival is held in Rio de Janeiro. Millions of people take part or go to watch. The streets are filled with brilliantly decorated floats and dancers dressed in spectacular costumes.

Countries

There are 12 countries in South America. There are also two small **territories**—French Guiana and the Falkland Islands.

CARIBBEAN SEA

Guyana

Venezuela

Suriname

French Guiana

Colombia

Ecuador

Brazil

Peru

Bolivia

Paraguay

PACIFIC OCEAN

ATLANTIC OCEAN

Uruguay

Chile

Argentina

N
W   E
S

0   500 miles
0   800 km

The Falkland Islands

This map shows the countries and territories of South America.

This photograph shows the government building in Brasilia, the capital of Brazil.

Brazil is the biggest country in South America. It is also the fifth largest country in the world. The smallest country in South America is Suriname. Brazil is about 50 times bigger than Suriname.

Cities and Countryside

In South America there are many cities where large numbers of people live. Among the biggest are São Paulo in Brazil and Buenos Aires in Argentina. São Paulo is busy and crowded. It has many modern buildings. It also has many **slums** where very poor people live.

Skyscrapers tower over the city of São Paulo, Brazil.

These children live in an Aymara village in a remote part of Peru.

Life in the countryside is very different. For example, the Aymara people live in villages in the Andes Mountains in Bolivia, Chile, and Peru. Often, the villages have no electricity or running water.

Fun Facts

- Angel Falls in Venezuela is the world's highest waterfall. The water plunges 3,212 feet (979 meters) down.

- About three-quarters of South America lies to the south of the **equator**.

- The Amazon rain forest in Brazil is about the same size as Australia.

- Lake Titicaca in Bolivia is the highest lake that boats can sail on.

Quiz

1. Which people built Machu Picchu in the Andes Mountains?

2. Which country in South America is very long and thin?

3. What is the world's longest mountain range?

4. What is the largest rain forest in South America?

4. The Amazon rain forest in Brazil

3. The Andes

2. Chile

1. The Inca people

Glossary

anaconda huge snake that lives in the rain forest
capybara animal that looks like a huge guinea pig
condor large bird that flies over mountains
continent one of seven huge areas of land on Earth
descended from related to someone long ago
equator imaginary line running around the middle of Earth
grasslands very large area of land covered in grasses
mined dug up from under the ground
mountain range long line of mountains
natural resources natural materials that we use, such as wood, coal, oil, and rock
ore rocks that contain metals
reeds tall grasses that grow in water or marshy land
slums overcrowded area of a city where poor people live
territories lands that are controlled by another country, far away
tropical place near the equator where the weather is hot and rainy all year

Find Out More

Books

Ganeri, Anita. *Exploring South America*. Chicago: Heinemann, 2007.

Gibson, Karen Bush. *Spotlight on South America*. Mankato, Minn.: Capstone, 2011.

Royston, Angela and Michael Scott. *South America's Most Amazing Plants*. Chicago: Raintree, 2009.

Web sites

FactHound offers a safe, fun way to find Internet sites related to this book. All of the sites on FactHound have been researched by our staff.

Here's all you do:
Visit www.facthound.com
Type in this code: 9781432980443

Index